"*Decisive parent* ful parents striving to raise virtuous children in today's world. Drawing on his years of experience as a father to his eleven children and as an educator at The Heights School, Michael Moynihan provides sound guidance on how successful parents forge strong character in their children. Full of practical advice, such as how parents can best navigate the challenges and opportunities associated with new technologies, the comprehensive approach Moynihan takes, using the four causes as his starting point, models to the reader how to best study his or her own family situation."

—Alvaro deVicente, Headmaster, The Heights School

"In a sea of 21st century parenting books that are heavily dependent on the newest ideas and 'research,' Moynihan offers a concise and refreshing return to commonsense parenting. Moynihan writes with the heart of a father and the insight of a scholar. Drawing from the wisdom of countless generations, *Decisive Parenting* is one of the only parenting books that is truly a must-read for sensible parents raising children in the modern world."

—Jeremy Tate: Founder, Classic Learning Test

"Amid a cacophony of conflicting voices on raising children, here is compelling advice on how to guide and nurture the young toward lives of faith, character, and contentment. Rooted in ancient wisdom and ordered toward virtue, Michael Moynihan's *Decisive Parenting* offers both sound philosophy and practical tools that serve the veteran parent as well as the first-timer. With clarity and humility, this longtime educator and father of eleven children reminds us of the need to parent decisively while finding delight in the process."

—Elisabeth Sullivan, Executive Director,
Institute for Catholic Liberal Education

"Mr. Moynihan has written just the book parents need to raise children who not only love what is true, beautiful and good, but who also have the self-mastery to attain it. The book is very readable and full of examples. During the twenty-three years I have taught Christian Anthropology, I have wished someone would write such a book. In addition, as a teacher of two of his children, I have witnessed the success of this method."

—Bonnie Hanssen, Faculty,
Theology Teacher, Oakcrest School

DECISIVE
Parenting

DECISIVE
Parenting

Forming
Authentic Freedom
in Your Children

MICHAEL MOYNIHAN

Scepter

Published by Scepter Publishers, Inc.
info@scepterpublishers.org
www.scepterpublishers.org
800-322-8773
New York

Cover design by Carol Cates
Book design and pagination by Rose Design

Library of Congress Cataloging-in-Publication Data available

Printed in the United States of America

Paperback ISBN: 9781594173417
eBook ISBN: 9781594173424

Contents

———— •◆• ————

Preface

———— • ◆ • ————

Most don't know how well they have done as parents until their children are in their thirties, though for some even that may be too early. But for those parents blessed with a clear vision of their mission in life and with cooperative children, this book can help them enjoy the fruits of their labor even in teenagers of age fifteen or sixteen.

Like many men, I enjoy reading books by great coaches, but even the greatest college coaches, like John Wooden, started their task with young men fairly well formed by their parents and teachers. No parent, however, gets to start where John Wooden began. Instead, parents are given a newborn: cute, but a demanding bundle of needs.

Many parents feel lost at sea regarding how to transform that newborn into the sixteen-year-old who has decided that his happiness depends on a life serving God and others. Michael Moynihan, a veteran teacher of boys and a father of eleven, expertly maps the journey.

In this book he lays out a clear guide:

- What virtues children have to acquire while young;
- How to put an everyday face on those virtues;
- How ordinary family life is rich in opportunities to live and teach these virtues;
- How much like a donkey their children are (stubborn and dumb), which mostly is fallen human nature;
- How to act when children wander or even refuse;
- How to spot 'personality-stifling' entertainment and how to let children in on the 'game' being played on them;
- How children provide parents with opportunities to nourish true freedom;
- How failures and wounds can be used to form prudence and wisdom;

- How children can spot the difference between freedom and its enemy, license;
- How humility is pivotal for everything good;
- How to nurture a reflective attitude.

What I suspect is the author's greatest achievement—literally Aristotelian, but without the philosophical heavy lifting—is how he helps parents to spot the four different causes at work in their children, and having identified them, to harness them repeatedly.

The book has other virtues. It will motivate parents on their own personal journey; some, because they are seeing a clear path for the first time.

This book, distilled from twenty-three years of forming virtue in his own children and in his pupils, points towards the next book, full of the stories that lie behind this one's wisdom. Maybe some parents will add their own stories to that volume.

—Pat Fagan, Ph.D.

Introduction

——— ·◆· ———

Most parents want their children to grow up to be caring people, responsible citizens, competent professionals, and loyal friends. They also hope their children embrace true moral principles and deeply practice their religious faith, internalizing a way of being that leads ultimately to happiness not only in this life but in the life to come. Such parents hope that their children go through this life with a spirit of service to others and as close friends of God.

My wife and I are no exception to this. As the parents of a rather large family—eleven children so far, ranging in age from one year to twenty years old—Angela and I, like all parents, make many sacrifices for our children in the hope that they in turn will grow into generous and self-sacrificing adults whose lives are rooted in a relationship with God. Though it is not easy, we know that the sacrifices are very much worth it, especially if they help our children develop into the men and women God wants them to be. For many years we felt a bit like soldiers in the thick of battle, not knowing if our efforts would pay off. It is a great joy now to see our older children becoming the young adults we have always hoped they would be.

My wife and I could never have made it this far without lots of help from others. I am very grateful for all of the experienced parents who have shared perspective and wisdom, especially the many dedicated and thoughtful parents affiliated with The Heights School, where I have worked for more than twenty years. The Heights School is distinctive for its mission to assist parents in helping their sons develop into close friends of God—and the leaders our world desperately needs. As head of the Upper School, I work with many families and have a privileged vantage point from which to see the impact of particular parenting decisions. Over the years, I have talked with parents who have realized they need to become more involved in their sons' lives in certain ways and others who have come to realize that they need to allow their sons more space to develop. These experiences, as well as my ongoing efforts to become classically educated myself, have helped me consider the topic of raising children from a unique perspective.

What follows is my attempt to reflect on how parents today can raise their children so that they are basically adults by the age of fifteen or sixteen. Granted, a fifteen-year-old cannot be ready to take on the full responsibilities of adulthood in our world today. Two hundred years ago, it may have been possible for a young man of seventeen to establish his own homestead and farm and marry a young woman of sixteen. But given the way the modern economy works, additional professional formation—likely involving years of college or other preparation—is necessary for someone to be ready to be on his or her own in the world.

So when I say that it is possible for persons as young as fifteen to be well-formed adults, I do not mean that they should actually shoulder the full responsibilities of married adult life in today's world. Rather, I mean that they can each have the character of an adult, capable of responsibly pursuing the proper course that his or her life should follow. They can be morally strong, ethically committed, and mature enough to actively forge their paths in life rather than aimlessly accepting whatever experiences come. They can each live a purposeful life that shows all signs of being a happy one on this earth, and, more importantly, one that is directed toward eternal happiness with God.

How can parents raise such children? This is not an easy question to respond to, mostly because there are no simple and short answers. But it is not an impossible question. There are answers. There is much that can be said about how parents can raise such children. We can study the problem of parenting today to gain perspective that will enable us to make better decisions.

It may not be entirely possible to objectively step back from the task of parenting today, as if we were foreigners visiting from another place or time. We are somewhat limited in our ability to do this because we are so close to the task at hand. It is not possible for us to be impartial observers of ourselves, and it is similarly difficult for us to step back from family life as it is lived today, seeking broader perspective. This is one reason why it is so helpful to discuss challenges with wise friends who can provide additional perspectives.

Even so, we are capable of calmly studying and reflecting upon the awesome task of raising children today: not perfectly, but certainly profitably. The key is to look at parenting from a comprehensive perspective. The Ancients had an outstanding way to do just this. Aristotle noted that to comprehensively understand something, it is helpful to look at what has caused it—and to do this in a fourfold sense. The principle of causality applies to everything. Nothing causes itself. All contingent things are caused by something other than themselves. And causality is present in four ways: material, formal, efficient, and final. This analysis, though perhaps not taught as clearly today as in times past, has been a key characteristic of western thought for centuries.

For a complete explanation of a thing, it is helpful to consider each of the four causes. We can consider the task of raising children to be God-centered—and other-centered—adults, and specifically the role of parents in this task, from the perspective of the four causes:

- The material cause is that *out of which* a thing comes to be. For our purposes we need to understand the matter we are working with; specifically, we need to understand what children are like.

- The formal cause is that *through which* a thing comes to be. Children become responsible adults of the type we are describing through acquiring the virtues. Parents need to help form their children in the four cardinal virtues—prudence, temperance, fortitude, and justice—as well as the theological virtues of faith, hope, and charity. Humility is also important, a great protector of other virtues.

- The efficient cause is that *by which* a thing comes to be. Children today face many influences, including at times significant negative pressures that work against the forging of strong characters. But the influence of parents can be decisive, and prudent parental decisions and actions can greatly help.

- The final cause is that *for which* a thing comes to be. Wise parents know that the goal is for their children to freely embrace a life lived in service to God and others. Freedom is key. Parents should foster authentic freedom in their children, never allowing them to settle for cheap imitations of the good that we all seek.

This book is written with young parents in mind. What would be helpful for a young parent to know as he or she considers all that raising children today entails? However, experienced parents can also benefit, profitably studying their particular family situations and deciding on practical ways to improve going forward. I have seen dedicated parents transform their families after a rough start.

Much of what follows is what I wish I would have known when I was a young parent. In my own family, I have only imperfectly lived what I write about here. There have been many occasions when my wife and I have had to apologize to our children for our mistakes and lack of prudent judgment. Know that if something you read leads you to regret how you have acted thus far, you are not alone; I have had the same experience in writing this.

A family is a communion of persons. And while each person is unique, we share a common humanity. Those who struggle to live noble human lives have similar internal challenges to overcome, even if the external circumstances are quite different. There are extraordinary individuals who have overcome very difficult upbringings in a truly heroic manner. There are also people who have turned against the values of a loving and God-centered family, despite the prayers and kindness of parents and siblings. When considering persons, we also must keep in mind that the element of human freedom is far from predictable.

My experience working with the many outstanding families in the Heights community has confirmed for me that there are no perfect families. Every family has difficulties, some lesser and some greater. Some of these difficulties are the result of decisions parents have made, and others are entirely outside parental control. Even the best parents typically have one or more blind spots, and some related suffering that calls for greater commitment and generosity.

But every parent has the potential to lovingly accept the family situation as it is and take steps to improve. We can take a step back and observe the general difficulties of parenting today, in our materialistic culture with all its present challenges. And we can consider our own particular family situations in light of these challenges—and raise our children accordingly.

CHAPTER ONE

———— •◆• ————

The Material Cause

WHAT CHILDREN ARE REALLY LIKE

The Beginning of the Adventure

It is with great joy that a young couple first discovers that they are expecting a baby. Perhaps this couple has recently married and is still getting used to living with each other and to the routines of married life. As they think about all the changes that this new life is bringing and will bring to their family, it's natural to feel some apprehension. Husband and wife are eager to meet the new baby in seven or eight short months, but also a bit unsettled by the prospect.

The coming of a new baby certainly will bring changes, including a new set of routines and a bit less (or perhaps significantly less) sleep.

A typical newborn's needs are fairly straightforward. The infant hopefully gets into a pattern of semi-regular eating and sleeping. At times he or she will cry, sometimes for a reason that parents can identify (tired, hungry, full diaper) and sometimes for no apparent discernible reason. My wife and I assign "trouble passing gas" as the reason for infant crying when the cause is not obvious. Though the discomfort associated with gas may be the problem a fair amount of the time, we readily admit that attributing a reason to the crying makes it easier to tolerate.

Soon the little one will be rolling around the carpet, crawling, walking, running, and climbing. The pint-sized explorer will likely be into all sorts of trouble as he or she discovers such places as the pantry and bathroom. Parents will find spilled flour in the kitchen and toothpaste artwork on the bathroom mirror. Despite these annoyances, the parents' lives will be full of great joy watching their toddler discover the world. They will laugh to see the world again through the eyes of a little child. My wife and I and our older children were recently highly amused by our two-year-old son's latest insight into the world around him. Patrick insists on calling every squirrel he sees a "monkey rabbit." Our older son Thomas notes that it is the perfect name for this tree-climbing creature with hand-like paws that bounds across the lawn.

Eventually parents get used to the routine of caring for their young child. There is a natural economy to the job of parenting a toddler: put lots of energy into caring for the little one and be richly rewarded by seeing him or her grow and learn about the world. The constant small sacrifices parents make help them to become more generous and other-centered. The growth of the child is accompanied by the parents' growth in patience and virtue. Most parents are very happy with this state of affairs.

The First Real Battle

And then comes the first clash of wills. I do not mean the first time a toddler is stopped from reaching for a pot of boiling water on the stove. In situations like this, the little one may cry at having his will momentarily contradicted by a loving mother grabbing his hand while emphatically saying, "No! Hot!" But such a toddler will be off on another quest in a few seconds, perhaps deciding to explore the contents of some lower kitchen cabinets.

What I mean by the first clash of wills is when a parent realizes for the first time that the child is mischievously defying his or her authority. Perhaps a three-year-old boy purposely and repeatedly slams his bedroom door after being told to settle down for his nap. In the room next door, the mom is frazzled trying to get his newborn baby sister to sleep. It becomes clear to the mom that her son understands the situation. In addition to simply not wanting to take a nap, he is getting back at his mom for leaving him in his bedroom while she spends time with his new sister. He knows that making this slamming noise is particularly upsetting to his mom, and this is precisely why he is doing it. He wants to be asked to stop, precisely because he can then keep slamming the door with deliberate purpose.

When faced with such willful defiance for the first time, sensible parents understand that it is not surprising that children behave this way. They know that in addition to having many wonderful qualities, children are also prone to being selfish and manipulative. This does not mean that there is not a beautiful innocence to children. Parents experience great joy at seeing the world through the eyes of their children largely because their childlike perspective can teach us how we have grown old in unhealthy ways.

But reflective parents know that being selfish and not acting in a virtuous manner is part of the story of our human condition. We are complicated creatures. We often do the evil thing that we hate (Romans 7:15). We experience ourselves as prone to selfishness and wrongdoing. If we are honest, we know that the child's door-slamming rebellion is mirrored in ourselves in various ways. All of us have been impacted by original sin.[1]

---

1. Each person has been wounded by sin, starting with original sin at the first moment of his or her existence in the mother's womb. Original sin is not just the sum total of the bad influences of society on a person who is flawlessly conceived. Original sin is not just bad socialization, a fallen society imposing

Sensible parents instinctively know this. They understand willful defiance for what it is, knowing that their child is prone to act badly at times. They also know that it is their responsibility to correct such defiance, so as to properly form their child to act rightly. A sensible response to the above door-slamming scenario would be to change the situation in some way. Perhaps the misbehaving boy should be firmly but calmly told he is out of line and then made to sit on the steps in silence, a temporary change in plan from the naptime routine. He has lost his privilege of having a normal naptime and must sit for a while in still silence before he is allowed to go back to his room for a nap, risking a more serious consequence if he disobeys. Corporal punishment as an initial response to the door slamming is not as effective since it is done in reaction to a situation primarily defined by the child; spanking would communicate to the child that he

---

its faults on an otherwise innocent and pure creature. The Council of Trent teaches that original sin is transmitted by generation (propagation) rather than by imitation. St. Thomas Aquinas understands original sin as the privation of sanctifying grace, a perfection that should be present had we not sinned in Adam. Though this privation is removed by baptism, the concupiscence, or disordered tendencies toward sin caused by original sin, remains.

has been effective in getting the situation out of the parent's control. Having the child sit quietly in reparation for what he has done with the known result of a more serious consequence if he fails to do this is different. The correction has been made, a proper calming medicine has been applied, and the situation is once again firmly in the parent's control.

The "Human Engineering Heresy"

It is difficult for many parents to maintain this sensible outlook today. When faced with children who misbehave, parents tend to blame themselves: "What have I done wrong to make my adorable child behave in this way?" Mothers in particular, especially if they are with their young children most of the time, might worry that they have failed to properly nurture their children and that this is the reason for the bad behavior. It is easy for a mother to become paralyzed by the situation, suffer internal anguish on account of her children, and not know what to do.

But if this happens, it is important that she be able to turn to her husband for support. He needs to be patient and reassuring, helping her to see the situation in perspective, primarily through being attentive to her. While he certainly can offer advice, he should not be too quick to think that what is needed is for him to "fix" the situation right away, especially if this happens when his wife is home with the children and he is at work. When home, he needs to actively back up his wife, letting his children know how much he loves their mother and insisting that they respect and obey her.

But there is more that should be said here. It is liberating for parents to identify the erroneous messages they receive today from multiple sources, messages that make it difficult for them to keep their good humor and common sense when faced with children being willfully defiant and misbehaving. We can summarize all these messages as contributing to what we can call the "human engineering heresy." This "heresy" involves some denial of the reality of sin, both original and personal, coupled with the notion that modern techniques of managing people can engineer proper behaviors. Jean-Jacques Rousseau was influential in articulating some of this thinking. He argued that people are born in a state of natural innocence that is in accord with virtuous action. Societal influences corrupt this natural innocence, leading to various vices.[2] Today parents are led to believe similarly that children are born perfect and learn bad behavior from society, which for young children basically means parents and a few others.

The marketing of baby products often presents an idyllic image of parenting, such as a mother and child smiling as they walk through a park holding hands. In various ways—from advertisers, books, and blogs—parents are told that the right diet, high in certain things and low in others, with organic ingredients, can positively impact behavior. More significantly, popular psychology presents positive reinforcement and proper management, along with a bit of introspective criticism of adult tendencies to think their children should be a certain way, as the key to engineering healthy behaviors. If a parent is positive and allows the child to "be

---

2. Notice the contrast between Rousseau's position and the Christian understanding of original sin and concupiscence.

himself," exploring who he is for himself within safe boundaries, then all will be well.

Granted—this narrative continues—there are bad influences in the world that do have an impact. But if we help children learn to express their feelings properly and show them how to politely get along with others, all in a carefully planned environment, then we will be able to keep the negative societal influences at bay. Parents need to be facilitators of desired behavior, which will naturally follow when they understand the perspectives of their children and help their children to understand others. So goes the narrative that unfortunately informs the way many well-intentioned parents view their children.

The human engineering heresy narrative complicates parenting, especially in how it can lead parents to doubt their worth and the importance of sensible adult leadership. Parents see themselves as failed nurturers, as failures in supporting their children's quest for self-discovery and self-expression. To the extent that parents buy into this muddled thinking, they will be extremely discouraged when faced with a door-slamming three-year-old son. The parents will naturally blame themselves for this problem.

So the first thing that parents need to know about children is that they are not perfect, partly because of immaturity but more fundamentally because of our fallen human condition. Though grace is effective and can even be transformative, the disordered tendencies that we have inherited will be with us throughout life. Even responsible adults experience the need for ongoing struggle against what is disordered within themselves. It should come as no surprise that in the case of children, misbehavior is not primarily something picked up from a fallen world, from parents who fail to nurture and protect them. Rather, we all carry within ourselves the wounds of sin and some of our actions directly arise out of a disordered heart.

Parents Need to Actively Exercise Leadership

This means that the first lesson parents need to learn is that they are meant to exercise loving authority over their children. Parents need to place reasonable demands and expect obedience. This is the fundamental point that is too often missed today. In fact, an argument could be made that the single greatest parenting mistake of our time is parents failing to provide proper leadership in their families. When parents believe some form of the human engineering heresy, they correspondingly assume that it is not their place to exercise authority.

But permissive parenting leads to mentally and emotionally unstable children. It is terrifying and potentially damaging to children to place them in positions where they need to take responsibility for aspects of life for which they are neither ready nor capable. But when parents lack confidence in their authority and fail to establish clear boundaries, they do just this.

Consider a boy who is used to getting his own way when he requests something. Sure, his parents will forbid him from doing anything dangerous, like playing with matches or lighting items on fire over the gas stove. But they allow him to watch mindless shows on TV or waste time playing video games, activities that parents know deep down are not noble and worthy of a virtuous and free person. Parents justify this to themselves by noting that the screens keep the child occupied and "out of trouble," as well as by the Rousseauian notion that the child likes this so it must be in some sense okay.

The child knows that these screens are not really good for him. After hours of such mind-numbing activity, he feels empty, recognizing the absence of the good that should have been present. He senses that his parents are really not right to be allowing him to do this. Though he cannot articulate it, he recognizes on some level the loss of his dignity in being allowed to "medicate" his boredom through such captivating entertainment. This is true even though he would forcefully rebel if his parents took the screens away from him, especially if the addictive pattern of drowning boredom through screen use is ingrained.

Similarly, children who are typically consulted as if they were adults will also pick up the idea that their parents do not really know what is best for them. If their parents routinely ask them if they are willing to do such things as go to visit grandma or take piano lessons, the children will assume that their parents are placing their children's preferences over what is objectively good. I am not advocating never asking children for their preferences; sometimes it is prudent to consult children in an age-appropriate way. But if children are raised in such a way that their parents rarely or never make purposeful decisions for their good, they will not internalize what is really objectively good. They will be trained to think that they need to determine for themselves what is good, which they know they are not able to do.

Sensible parents make parental decisions based primarily on what is objectively good for their children rather than relying excessively on their children's preferences. They place reasonable demands on their children, including assigning specific, regular chores and requiring age-appropriate acts of service throughout the day. They confidently tell their children to help the family or others in specific ways and expect them to do so.

Children Can Remind Parents What Reality Is Really Like

Up to this point, we have emphasized that children are very much works in progress, that they need guidance and even discipline to properly grow. We specifically rejected the Rousseauian ideal of children being born into a pure, natural state and then corrupted by societal influences, noting that this narrative fails to understand the reality of our human condition.

But there is another side to what children are like. Alongside their tendency to manipulative door-slamming and such, there is also an openness and simplicity in children that is sadly lacking in many adults. Jesus refers to this when he scolds his apostles and insists that the children should be allowed to come to him, even noting that it is necessary to receive the kingdom of God like a little child in order to be able to enter it. Jesus knows that many adults have become old in unhealthy ways, internalizing a jaded view of reality. Perhaps they see the world in overly "practical" ways, as a harsh place where street smarts are necessary to fight for a share of the "good life." Another "adult problem" is allowing scientism to inform one's worldview. Those who do this tend to see material reality as nothing more than a set of passive construction units functionally arranged in mechanical configurations. In either case, those lacking a proper moral vision and those prone to reductionism share the same underlying problem: they have stripped reality of transcendence. This leads to jaded adults who fail to see that creation is good and, along with the moral order, points ultimately to the source of all good, God himself.

Children, by contrast, are born realists, meaning that they are naturally disposed to understanding reality as it is presented to them. Inward-looking idealist conceptions of reality are foreign to them. Children are profoundly interested in the natural world. When they first start to learn how to talk, they will repeat over and over the names of things, asking their parents to "Look!" and see the bird, tree, mountain, water, or whatever. Repetition that is tedious to adults is exciting to young children. They continue to see the mystery of *being* present again and again in the same things. They ask for the same book to be read immediately after it is finished.

Adults find this somewhat amusing but also tiring. Part of this is natural: a healthy adult contemplation of reality involves more than finding joy in the same thing over and over again. But part of what is going on is that adults have been influenced negatively by our materialistic culture. Adults tend to see mystery, for example, as something to be explained away rather than contemplated. To an adult, a mystery is too often merely a puzzle to be solved, comprehended, and then conveniently set aside until it has a use. Knowing about gravity, an adult is less amazed that water runs downhill. A child, on the other hand, sees the brook as truly enchanted. Granted, the child's view is simple, but it is also arguably more correct inasmuch as he or she better appreciates the *being* that is there.

And reality really is rich in transcendent meaning. The beauty and goodness of creation point toward the moral order and the broa purpose that surrounds each human life. Tolkien once described his *Lord of* trilogy as an antidote to modernity. He specifically wrote these works for his children, to educate them in a more correct and noble way of viewing reality. To take just one example, at the Council of Elrond, the wise come to the conclusion that, rather than use the ring as a powerful but dangerous weapon against the enemy, they must take it secretly into Sauron's domain and destroy it. This decision arguably only makes sense when one believes in a deeper purpose that is guiding all of history, a belief in divine providence. And so, some of our own moral choices only make sense from a broader perspective that takes into account more than the ends we can calculate. We do what is right because a transcendent moral order actually exists and our role is to humbly follow what is right, despite difficult consequences that may follow. We seek personally to serve others and believe in the necessity of the warmth of human charity, knowing that purely efficient solutions to the world's problems are ultimately inadequate.

Children are able to teach adults important lessons about reality, often in a natural and pleasant way. Adults love to share childlike delight in things, from the water in the brook to the clouds in the sky. Parents relive their own childhood on Christmas Eve as they get everything ready for the little ones to discover the next day. They also are constantly amused at seeing their children learn about the world around them. The observations of little children are at times priceless.

So one of the great joys of parenting is seeing the world from the fresh and simple perspective of one's children. This leads to some practical conclusions:

- Lead strongly but with humility. As parents provide strong leadership and loving discipline, they should keep in mind that their main purpose should be to serve their children by helping them stay true to the right path. Even when making necessary and painful corrections, parents should be cognizant of the great goodness that exists in their children, confident that discipline can help redirect them to act in accord with their true nature. If parents are mindful of their role to serve what is objectively good when they administer discipline, the result will be to strengthen their children's ideals and commitment to the good. It is a great thing to be able to enter adulthood with one's childhood ideals still intact.

- Spend time outside. Young children love to be around nature, and parents should make time to go for walks with them. A particular favorite is a creek expedition, where parents and children wear old shoes and hike along a creek bed. Parents can join their children in learning the names of various plants, animals, and birds.

- Never lie to children. Children are inclined to trust what their parents tell them. This trust is closely tied to a fundamental confidence that reality is good and that living for noble ideals is worthwhile. It is never acceptable to lie to anyone. But there is a sense in which telling the truth to children is particularly important. Lying to children can deform their worldview and corrupt their ideals, threatening their very understanding of reality. Some parents regularly tell lies to their children and think nothing of it. They may tell lies of convenience like, "The candy is all gone. No more." Or tell lies to try to comfort them like, "Your dog Fido is now in heaven with God. You will see him again." Telling the truth does not mean that parents cannot tell stories to children. Fairy tales and other fiction stories can be powerfully formative, often teaching lessons about deep and transcendent aspects of reality. And not all questions children ask need to be answered. Sensible parents realize this and can balance being playful and appealing to the imagination—an important way to convey some truths about reality— with the need to convey accurate facts. Even so, sensible parents will not consider playfulness as an excuse for inappropriate types of deception. When dealing with Santa Claus, for example, my wife and I allow the children to believe what they want as a sort of game without ever telling them that Santa is real. Sometimes we tell the real story of St. Nicholas, the bishop who upheld the orthodox faith in the face of the Arian heresy and gave to the poor. I enjoy asking my young children who they think Santa Claus is and then replying with something like, "What! You mean to tell me that he is going to break into our house and take our cookies and carrots? He must be stopped!" They know I am joking and laugh heartily. But the important point comes across: believing in Santa Claus is a fun thing for children to do and is distinct from important matters like belief in God.

In short . . .

Parents need to see children in a realistic way. They are neither little angels who can do no wrong nor little brutes who need to be forcefully tamed. They are self-centered and prone to seek to gratify their appetites and passions. They are capable of manipulating others to get what they want. But they also are innocent, at least initially, of reductive and materialistic patterns of thinking that are typical of adults today. Fundamentally, children are very much in need of being educated and formed in the right way. Actually, we all can benefit from ongoing study and formation, specifically continuing to reflect and seek advice on family life and our growth in virtue. This need for guidance is just more obvious in the case of children.

CHAPTER TWO

———— •❖• ————

The Formal Cause

THE VIRTUES

A strong character is precisely what differentiates a responsible adult from a child; it is through the development of character that a child becomes a responsible adult. Character is the sum total of the inner strengths that enable one to live a noble human life, a life oriented toward serving God and others in integrity and truth. Character is forged through acquiring virtues, which are stable habits that enable one consistently to act in a noble way. Thus the virtues are the formal cause—that through which something comes to be—of a child entering responsible adulthood.

Virtues are good habits, stable dispositions that enable people to act correctly, oftentimes with ease. We all know what bad habits are and how people are prone to act in certain ways by their bad habits. People who habitually crack their knuckles may end up doing so during a class in a half-thinking way. They probably do not intentionally want to disrupt class but, giving in to the force of habit, end up doing so. Being prone to outbursts of anger is a more deep-seated character flaw, a habitual tendency to overreact to annoyances and lose one's temper.

In contrast, as good habits, virtues make it easier for people to act nobly and for the good. Prudent people habitually consider different ways to accomplish a particular goal and choose an excellent course of action, even anticipating some potential difficulties that may arise. Persons of faith adhere to the truth about God and our human condition and history. They see the great struggles of our time as part of a broader narrative, a real story with meaning and a victory that is both already present and continuing to be realized.

The virtues can be divided into the four cardinal virtues—prudence, temperance, fortitude, and justice; the three theological virtues of faith, hope and charity; and the protective virtue of humility. There are other virtues that can be mentioned—such as industriousness, patience, and kindness, to give just a few examples. These other virtues, however, are more specific aspects of the cardinal and theological virtues and humility.

Virtues are not going to remove the effects of original sin. Virtuous people will continue to struggle with rebellious appetites and various other inner complications that are part of our human condition on this side of the grave. But the acquisition of the virtues does help. Acquiring virtues helps both to give an overall orientation toward a noble life and to make following this path easier. Virtues can also help people to recognize their shortcomings and take the practical steps necessary to make course corrections, especially if they are prudent enough to seek counsel from others. Each one of us is prone to blindness about our own faults and situations, at times lacking perspective that is obvious to an outside observer.

Here are the specific virtues that contribute to a strong character:

- Theological Virtues—virtues that are infused at Baptism and grow especially through prayer, receiving of the sacraments, and exercising these virtues through acts. They are:

  - Faith—belief in God and in all that he has revealed through his Church;
  - Hope—confidence that God is a loving Father who will give us the means to eternal salvation; and
  - Charity—a love for God that leads us to love and serve others. True charity is much more than mere philanthropy: the love of God is primary, ordering and determining all other loves and affections toward this greatest of all loves.

- Cardinal Virtues—natural virtues recognized by the ancients well before the time of Christ. These virtues are strengthened and deepened by grace. They are:

- Prudence—sound judgment, an ability to make important distinctions that lead us to properly order our lives and make good, practical decisions on a regular basis. A prudent person habitually distinguishes good from evil, truth from falsehood, the important from the trivial, and the eternal from the transitory;

- Temperance—self-control, an ability to overcome "feelings" for the sake of a higher good, an ability to use pleasurable things moderately and reasonably, and rational control of the appetites;

- Fortitude—personal toughness, an ability to endure or overcome pain, discomfort, inconvenience, and disappointment for the sake of a noble goal; and

- Justice—a sense of responsibility, giving others their due, starting with God.

• Humility—recognizing the truth about God, ourselves, and creatures so as to actively know that on our own there is not much of true value that we can accomplish, but that with God, great things are possible. Humility is knowing that God is the chief author of any good that we are able to accomplish and that we owe all to him.

The job of parents is to instill these virtues in their children and to collaborate with others who can help in the formation of children in these virtues. Prudent parents know that this task is by far a parent's most important work. Parents provide for other needs of their children, and rightly so. Children need enough to eat, adequate shelter, medical care, and instruction that will enable them to enter the workforce so as to provide for others. But wise parents know that the best preparation they can possibly give their children, for both life and eternity, is to help them grow into men and women of character. People who live the virtues have the best possible preparation to serve others through rewarding professional careers and, more importantly, to serve their own families and God throughout their lives.

Virtues and the Moral Imagination

People acquire virtues primarily through act-ing in virtuous ways. Fortitude grows when one repeatedly chooses to do the good in spite of challenges, particularly challenges that involve some personal hardship. Such a person will be used to enduring hardships to accomplish the good. Acquiring virtue is fundamentally a per-sonal matter, a matter that must involve a free, personal choice. Without freedom, it is not pos-sible to grow in virtue. So there is a sense in which it is not possible for a parent or anyone else to form virtue in a child. The virtue will only take root when the child decides to act vir-tuously. More on the topic of freedom follows in chapter 4.

But parents can help form their children in virtue in two ways: by directed practice and by presenting a compelling vision of virtuous action that expands the child's moral imagination. Directing children to practice virtue happens in specific situations, in the natural ebb and flow of family life. Parents establish a home in a par-ticular way, plan a family schedule, and respond to the various situations that emerge in family life. These parental decisions are best considered under the aspect of the parents' role as efficient cause, in the next chapter.

Here we will focus on the role of parents in expanding the moral imaginations of their children so that they understand the virtues as attractive and see the beauty of each virtue in a well-lived life. The moral imagination refers to the ideals that inform how a person understands what it means, for him or her personally, to strive to live a noble life dedicated to the good. A person with a well-developed moral imagination will see how growing in virtue will help him or her to become a great man or woman, someone who can have a tremendous positive impact. Inspired by the example of King Arthur, for example, the owner of a company may strive to lead with fortitude and prudence and be kind, faithful, and just in all dealings with his or her employees. Parents expand the moral imaginations of their children by teaching about the virtues. They do this by exposing children to the right stories and by talking with them about how the virtues are lived. At the right time, a parent will place a vision of living a particular virtue before a child, highlighting the particular path that he or she can follow.

- Stories. From the youngest age, parents should actively govern what stories children receive. Parents should choose stories rich in human meaning that take place against the backdrop of a moral universe. Sensible parents prefer the time-tested tales of Mother Goose over the drivel of other meaningless picture books. Many classic fairy tales also do an excellent job of presenting a world where virtue and the moral law are of transcendent value. Tolkien's *The Lord of the Rings* trilogy (the books, not so much the movies) presents multiple examples of heroic virtue and a deep insight into human nature, as does C.S. Lewis' *The Chronicles of Narnia* (again, the books do so much better than the movies). If children read and hear the right stories, powerful examples of virtue will take root in their souls.

- Connections. Parents should also actively make connections between the virtues children hear about in stories and how these virtues are lived today. This type of instruction should be a natural part of conversations. "That person is as loyal a friend as Master Samwise was to Mr. Frodo." "He leads with a real spirit of service—like Aragorn, who knows that the power of the king is meant for the good of his people." In this natural way, parents will help their children ponder what type of story they are living.

- Naming the virtues. A story often leaves a strong impression on a child. Hearing about the brave knight who saved the village from the threatening dragon awakens a child's longing for heroic and generous service. But this impression of heroic goodness quickly begins to fade, at times lasting only as long as the noble sentiments aroused by the story. The impression of goodness weakly endures as an emotional memory, difficult to hold onto over time. What is needed is more rational content to solidify the experience.

Naming the virtues displayed in a story helps to sharpen one's grasp of why a particular story is good. It adds solidity and endurance to the virtue. The knight is courageous, just like the police officer answering a call for help in a difficult neighborhood. Both are willing to sacrifice themselves for the good of those they protect.

• Modeling the virtues. Children tend to grow up to be like their parents. As a teacher, I have a privileged vantage point from which to observe this. It is striking how a few weeks after the school year begins, at back to school night, I stand before a classroom of parents whose mannerisms closely resemble those of their sons. More significantly, over time I observe how children grow up practicing the same virtues that are so impressive in their parents. Unfortunately, this also tends to be the case with vices. Children notice almost everything about their parents. They see our strengths and our weaknesses. They know when we are practicing heroic patience and kindness and when we are cold and selfish. They know whether we truly have hearts of service, focused on God and others, or if we are too overly impressed with the street smarts that can lead to getting ahead in the world. They know what is truly important to us: whether our focus is on caring for persons or possessing things. Though it may not seem like it at times, children slowly internalize the worldview of their parents. They also come to approach situations in the world outside their families in ways that are consistent with how they have seen their parents interacting with others. This happens even with children who are rebellious at home. They may challenge parents in the home for various reasons, but in interacting with the outside world, they are remarkably like their parents. Some teenage rebellion is a natural process of separation, but often one that tends to lead to adults who are similar to their parents. Thus perhaps the most important thing parents can do to help their children become virtuous adults is to work on growing in virtue themselves. Parents who know they are not perfect and are actively striving to live virtue tend to raise their children best.

———— •◆• ————

CHAPTER THREE

The Efficient Cause

DECISIVE PARENTING

P arents are the primary educators of their children. This means not only that parents are the first teachers but also that the job of educating their children is fundamentally their responsibility throughout the formative years of childhood. Parents may partner with schools to help in the formation of their children, but they continue to play a direct role through their example, in how they govern their home, by their parenting decisions and, hopefully, through direct teaching of certain matters as well. All of this is another way to say that the parents' role as part of the efficient cause of the development of their children is significant.

Children learn virtue by being presented with an attractive ideal that they seek to emulate, an ideal that informs their moral imaginations, and also by directed practice. Directed practice includes assisting children in doing things well. It can be as simple as teaching industriousness through having a child help Mom or Dad with chores. When I was young and growing up in rural upstate New York, my father would take me into the forest behind our house to help him cut firewood to heat our home. It was hard work, but I am truly grateful for those hours spent chopping wood. I learned much about work and service laboring alongside my father. Many years later, when I was an adult, I had a conversation with my father about this. He was surprised to hear that I considered it such a positive, formative experience. He had worried that perhaps he had expected too much from me, that perhaps he had "taken too much away" from my childhood. It was good to be able to sincerely thank him for disregarding my complaints at the time, something he probably would not have done if our family had not really needed my help to heat the house.

Directed practice is broader than direct parental assistance in completing tasks. Any structure or system parents use to govern the running of their household or family life is a type of directed practice. Children learn that there are times for meals, family reading, prayer, study, and sleep. Children learn a way of being, an internal ordering of their hearts, from how family life is lived.

For young children, the role of parents in forming virtue is fairly straightforward. As children get a bit older, the dynamic changes, although the role of parents is still critically important. Below are ways parents help children develop specific virtues through dealing with everyday situations:

- Food and meals. *Temperance*. Most young children tend to crave sweets and simple carbohydrates. They will ask for juice or some other sweet beverage. They tend not to want to eat vegetables. It can be difficult to get young children to eat food high in protein. It is easy to see how much children need parents to step in and limit their intake of sweets and junk food, requiring them to eat a more balanced selection of foods. Left to their own desires, their intemperance toward sugar could form a pattern for more serious intemperate or even addictive behaviors in the future. Children allowed to indiscriminately indulge their cravings will potentially be more prone to future intemperance with substances such as alcohol and will have a more difficult time developing the strength to guard their hearts in the face of the onslaught of sensual images present today. Parents appropriately exercise authority by expecting young children to eat at least a small amount of nutritious foods that they find distasteful. One way to do this is to serve a small amount of each item as a first helping at meals. Once the children eat everything on their plates, they can request more of what they want to eat. Likewise, children who do not eat their vegetables should know that they will not be permitted to have dessert. After a family meal, a child should ask for permission to be excused from the table. The normal expectation should be for everyone to linger around the table for a while, talking. After this can be a good time to begin chores as a family.

- Activity. *Temperance*. Many young children are also intemperately prone to activity. It is normal that children like to go from one activity to the next. Part of this comes from a healthy sense of excitement at being alive and enjoying play. But there is a need for parents to somewhat temper this energy, even if it is fundamentally a good thing. Without any structure to their days, children will go from one thing to the next until they finally collapse in exhaustion (which can take a remarkably long time!). Parents do well to structure some down time, in which even young children who have outgrown their naps still have an early afternoon "quiet time." Likewise, it is good for parents to direct their children to clean up after themselves before going on to another activity. Very young children may not be able to clean up their messes, but if they can pause to help Mom or Dad clean up, that is a good, small break in their activity. Otherwise they might serve as a force of disorder and destruction, leaving chaos in their wake.

- Encourage very little children in their desires to "help." *Charity, service, and industriousness.* Little children at times are eager to help their parents. A three-year-old may feel honored to be able to hand his or her father a tool during a household repair. A child may also want to help Mom cook something. Oftentimes this "help" involves more work for the parent. A striking image of this is a father holding his two-year-old son with one arm, allowing him to grab the handle of the push lawnmower now propelled by the one free hand of the father. The lad thinks of himself as helping his father, although it is really more work for his dad. I sometimes wonder if the way God set up the economy of salvation, allowing us to participate in his perfect sacrifice for the redemption of the world,[1] is not like this. But the son carried by his father does contribute one thing: he moves his father's heart by his desire to help. So we too may actually do very little efficient work for God, but our small sacrifices done with love are a way to enter into the heart of God. Allowing very young children to participate in their parents' work starts to build habits of industrious service. It communicates to children that we are all called to purposeful work. On the contrary, if a parent regularly sends a willing helper away for the sake of efficiency, that parent communicates to his or her child a reductive understanding of work that places efficiency above all else.

- Parents should direct children to specific acts of service, beginning when they are very young. *Charity, service, and industriousness.* Even two-year-old children can be asked to

---

1. Colossians 1:24 "Now I rejoice in my sufferings for your sake, and in my flesh I complete what is lacking in Christ's afflictions for the sake of his body, that is, the Church" (Revised Standard Version)

carry something to help Mom or Dad. At times they will want to do this, as when groceries are brought into the house and older siblings are helping. At other times, it is good for a parent to ask for help. As children get older, more should be asked of them. A four-year-old can be asked to put a toy away in its place on a shelf. Good chores for young children include transferring the clean silverware from the dishwasher basket to the silverware drawer, picking up toys, making their beds, and even performing daily tasks such as brushing their teeth.

- Family schedule. *Temperance, prudence, and order*. Young children thrive when there is a structure to the day. Much of this happens naturally, with times for meals, play, prayer, rest, listening to stories being read, and various other things. In our home, we have found it helpful to post a family schedule on the refrigerator on a daily basis. The schedule indicates times for family events as well as activities and tasks for specific family members. The schedule also indicates the times of unstructured free time, time that children should be encouraged to use well without overmanaging them. Having this structure helps children to internalize a sense of living order, of following a well-thought-out plan for the day. The eventual goal is for the children to grow up with the habit of calmly and reflectively studying a situation, pondering the most prudent course of action.

- Practiced times of silence. *Temperance, fortitude, contemplation, and patience.* Parents can promote contemplative reflection in their children by encouraging times of silence or even more reflective activities such as reading together. An afternoon quiet time, posted on the family schedule, is an excellent way to promote a break from activity, good reading habits, and the practice of study—and it even lays the groundwork for mental prayer and contemplation. An excellent way that children learn patience is to sit quietly through a service at church. If your child aged three or under is quiet in church, be very thankful, for there is not much you can do if he or she really wants to make noise! It amuses my wife and me when someone compliments us for a two-year-old behaving at church. We know how precarious the behavior of a two-year-old is and how little control we have over it. There does come a time when children are able to behave in church, and at that age parents should expect proper behavior. Several years ago, one of our children, then about age six, refused to sit with the family at church. He was making some commotion, clearly being willfully defiant. When we arrived home, we told him we were disappointed in how he behaved and that he needed to practice behaving the way he should in church so he would be better able to do so in the future. We then had him sit in a wooden chair in a corner, in silence, to help him build up the proper habit of how he should behave. His future behavior in church was much improved.

• Bedtime. *Temperance and prudence.* Parents should set bedtimes for their children and expect them to settle down in a reasonable way. An observant parent will know the difference between the child who needs some extra attention (being tucked in one more time, hearing that story again . . .) and the child who is manipulating the situation to try to avoid going to bed. When children are a bit older, parents can institute a time we refer to as "books or bed." In our house, this means that children have to leave the common areas and go to their bedrooms or just outside their bedrooms if someone is already asleep in there. The expectation is that they can quietly read until they are ready to retire for the night. After books or bed is called, the children are allowed to read or go to sleep; conversation and games come to an end. Some days we have a preset time for books or bed, perhaps 8:30 p.m. on a typical school night. On other days, books or bed is spontaneously called by a parent at some point in the evening.

- Toughness. *Fortitude*. Young children tend to be fairly soft and lazy. They lack the strength of will characteristic of a responsible adult. While taking a walk, three-year-olds may ask to be carried because they are tired. Parents do well to expect their children to keep up walking within reason (sometimes it is fine to carry them). An excellent way to develop fortitude is to take slightly older children on a hike up a mountain. The natural goal of reaching the top will motivate the children to work to conquer their tiredness. Sports are another tremendous means to build toughness and fortitude in children. Both boys and girls will respond to a good coach who encourages them to push themselves harder than they thought possible. For many children, the fortitude needed to persevere in studying and other school work is best developed precisely through learning to conquer themselves by fighting through the pain of a difficult workout, or overcoming nerves before a competition. Chores and manual labor can also help develop fortitude.

I learned a great deal about toughness, as well as service, by working alongside my father cutting, splitting, moving, and stacking the firewood.

- "It's not fair!" *Justice*. Children do not seem to have a problem understanding the need for justice. Indeed, they often loudly assert their right to a fair share. But justice is not only about knowing what one deserves. It is also about giving others what they deserve. Children's deficient understanding of justice is at times closer to a sense of entitlement. Children look for reasons why parents or others owe them things. If children ask inappropriately for what they think is their fair share of something, there are different ways a parent can respond. The worst way is to give the children what they want so they do not make a fuss. This is teaching children that whining and complaining or even the threat of doing so is helpful for them to get their own way. A better response is to refuse them—even though this means that annoying complaints are likely to follow. At times, a more creative and instructive response might be helpful. A parent could mention that it is not fair that a specific child has a messy room because this contributes to items being difficult to find or even broken, and that the family counts on everyone "taking good care of what we have." The parent might explain, "It is not a good idea to talk about getting what you want until your room is clean." Or the parent may simply mention how it is not fair that others in the family work hard on a task and, correspondingly, there is a chore that the child can do to help make up for his or her lack of fairness to the family. The parent might say, "Finish this task and then we can talk about what you want."

- Parents should take an active role in educating their children. *Studiousness and prudence.* When children start to read and write, parents should expect them to practice reading and writing at home. Parents are the primary educators of their children. Schools only educate with the permission and delegated authority of the parents. It is quite fitting that parents actively exercise their educative duty, at least from time to time. It is particularly fitting for parents to require their children to follow time-tested classical education methods that have fallen out of use at most schools. Parents should read aloud to their children, require children to memorize poetry or even prose passages, practice math problems, and even encourage children to copy well-chosen sentences, paragraphs, or poems. Modern progressive educational methods abandon these more traditional means. Today in most schools, creative or formulaic writing is emphasized to the exclusion of the imitation of excellent writing. This does a great disservice to our children. The first steps in learning how to write well are developing good reading habits, memorizing poetry and short prose selections, and copying by hand well-chosen passages. This copywork helps children to internalize by imitation a sense of what good writing is like. As children grow older, they can be asked to imitate a particular author's style in retelling a tale or even to answer a particular question as if they are one of the characters in a novel. Then the children will eventually be ready to write their own prose and poetry.

Screens

Sensible parents know that they need a well-thought-out plan to deal properly with the prevalence of media screens today. In many homes, TV, computer, video, and handheld screens are a significant or even determining factor in how family life is lived. For many people, near-constant connectivity through screens has become an integral part of how they live their lives. Many parents are uncomfortable with this status quo but are not sure what the proper parental response should be. There is a need to study the challenges and possibilities screens provide so as to be better able to make prudent parental decisions.

First of all, the technology behind the explosion of screens in the modern world has many positive aspects. Screens can contribute to human flourishing if they are used in the right way. The Internet provides a powerful means to communicate and access information. This facility in communicating and accessing information helps many professionals to be of greater service, saving time that previously was spent doing tasks in less efficient ways. Families can watch enriching films together. A favorite for our family is the Arts and Entertainment version of Jane Austen's *Pride and Prejudice*. Formed.org is an excellent site for many family-friendly movies. Screens can help facilitate access to cultural riches that would be unimaginable to our ancestors.

The challenge is that screens are difficult to use without becoming addicted, especially for young people. The brain of a young child, teen, and even young adult is wired to become more independent and self-sufficient, a process that necessitates exploration and learning.[2]

---

2. Beatriz Luna and Catherine Wright, "Adolescent Brain Development: Implications for the Juvenile Justice System," eds. K. Heilbrun, D. DeMatteo, and N.E.S. Goldstein, *APA Handbook of Psychology and Juvenile Justice* (Washington, DC: APA Publications, 2015), pp. 91–116, *APA PsycNET, dx.doi. org/10.1037/14643-005.*

However, the prefrontal cortex, which aids one's ability to practice self-control and minimize inappropriate risk-taking, is still developing in a young brain, a fact researchers continue to note, debating the implications.[3]

Modern family life is often negatively impacted by the presence of screens. People sit in the same room staring at their devices rather than interacting with one another in human ways. The prevalence of videos and video games has pushed out reading and even habits of deep, reflective thought and prayer. Social media consumption leads to many superficial interactions that are not in accord with authentic friendship. And numerous studies have shown that frequent use of social media is a contributing factor to mental illness, notably depression.[4]

---

3. D. Romer, V.F. Reyna, and T.D. Satterthwaite, "Beyond Stereotypes of Adolescent Risk Taking: Placing the Adolescent Brain in Developmental Context," *Developmental Cognitive Neuroscience* (October 27, 2017), pp. 19–34. Accessed on PubMed.gov, *https://www.ncbi.nlm.nih.gov/pubmed/28777995*.

4. See: *https://www.npr.org/2017/12/17/571443683/the-call-in-teens-and-depression*.

Sensible parents are uncomfortable with the downsides of screen use but also recognize that simply forbidding all screen use among their children is neither practical nor desirable. It is obvious that screen use needs to be limited and focused toward certain goods and that parents are the ones chiefly responsible for governing the use of screens in their family. Parents need to have a well-thought-out approach to screen use. Considering this from the perspective of the virtues is a good starting point:

- Studiousness. The virtue of studiousness entails the ability to concentrate on a particular course of study, persevering without giving in to distractions. A studious person is able to do what Cal Newport calls "deep work," by which he means sustained mental effort aimed at accomplishing a significant task.[5] Traditionally, the virtue of studiousness was defined in relation to the vice of curiosity. This is somewhat confusing today

---

5. Cal Newport, *Deep Work: Rules for Focused Success in a Distracted World* (New York: Grand Central Publishing. 2018).

since many people think of curiosity as a
virtue. What they really mean is that it is
good that a person is interested in learning
something about reality, as opposed to being
so intellectually dull that he or she is unin-
terested in acquiring knowledge. It is typical for a virtue to be a mean between two
extremes. Studiousness can rightly be seen
as the mean between someone whose intel-
lectual efforts are dissipated on many topics
or activities and who is unable to focus on
one long enough to achieve mastery (curiosity) and a dull boredom that sees reality
as profoundly uninteresting (acedia). It is
striking that the latter extreme has become
so prevalent today that it has made the for-
mer vice of curiosity seem like a virtue in
comparison.[6] The question parents need
to ask about their children's use of screens
is whether the screens are helping develop
studiousness or contributing to dissipated

---

6. I have filled out college recommendation forms that have asked me to
rate students in their curiosity, by which the author of the form meant a virtue
by which someone is interested in learning things.

thought and short attention spans. A person thinks through a process involving simple apprehension, judgment, and inference. The senses perceive an object that then is converted into a mental image. The intellect then abstracts from the mental image a concept through which the thing is known. Judgments are formed and rational reflection begins, a process that takes time. When reading a novel, a person forms a mental image of the scenes and then ponders these images at a measured and human pace. Watching a video is different. The screen provides the intellect with a series of images that dictate the pace at which the person will process the information. Likewise, the images are engineered to elicit certain emotional responses. A key implication is that not all videos are the same. Parents need to be discerning as to what they and their children watch. A Civil War documentary is not at all like a film that attempts to draw the audience in through rapidly changing scenes and a soundtrack that is designed for emotional impact. When evaluating a particular film, a parent should ask how this film is intended to be received by the viewer. Many good parents are careful to check for immoral content but are not thinking in terms of phenomenological impact. Regarding cell phones in particular, constant connectivity can lead to problems studying. Academic work can be significantly disrupted by text messages if the phone is nearby.

- Inner silence, patience, and a contemplative spirit. It is good for every person to spend some time in reflective thought. Whether it is sitting on the front porch in the afternoon, looking at the stars from the back deck in the evening, or taking a walk through the park, some down time is good for everyone. There are certainly uses of screens that are consistent with an appropriate amount of inner silence. Someone could read Scripture on a phone during a time of prayer or read a novel on an e-reader. And some accessing of information or entertainment can be an appropriate part of a balanced life. But these positive uses of screens tend to be planned rather than part of an ongoing habitual mode of living life connected to screens. It is problematic when a person is so attached to a constant stream of information that he or she is uncomfortable being disconnected.

- Being a sovereign knower, and personal integrity. In his profound essay *The Loss of the Creature*, Walker Percy, writing in the 1970s, highlights the problem that people in the modern age seek validation from outside experts rather than trusting their own abilities to know as sovereign knowers. A tourist in Percy's time inappropriately seeks outside validation that his experience of another culture is authentic while a student has a difficult time learning for himself rather than following a formulaic experience defined by educators. Today the situation is more challenging. Social media in particular has made it more difficult for people to even have authentic experiences.

The online world of the images of experiences is what many look to for validation of an experience. If it is not posted on social media, then it in some way lacks reality. At stake here is a person acting out of freedom, trusting that his or her experience of reality can be authentic. The need for some type of virtual validation of experience has left some people, especially young people, with a profound lack of self-confidence. What for Percy was a loss of a person's ability to understand the creature without expert validation has become for some of today's teens a loss of confidence in themselves as knowers, a surrender to the group so as to know themselves only as members of this collective.

- Charity. Charity is a gift of oneself to another, whether through some act of service or simply through being present to the person, listening with a loving attitude. The warmth of human charity is not something that easily comes through an interaction mediated by a screen. Sure, a young girl can write her grandmother a quick note through email or social media to let her know that she is thinking of her. It is not impossible to convey human warmth through a brief note sent over the Internet. But it is certainly helpful—and, in many cases, even necessary—to be fully present to another person to live charity. It is also necessary to possess oneself in order to be able to make an authentic gift of self. If a person has been conditioned to give up sovereignty to a group, it will be difficult for him or her to have the inner strength to love in a human way. So, in addition to the potential for making human interactions more superficial, the loss of personal integrity or sovereignty is another risk associated with some uses of screens, and especially some types of social media.

• Efficiency. Computers enable all of us to work more efficiently if they are used well. Students can profitably use computers to research, better edit their papers, communicate with classmates and teachers, and even organize their schedules (although a handwritten planner generally works quite well). The challenge, especially for young people, is to use the computer as a professional tool rather than to be manipulated by it. Social media companies hire experts to study how they can get people to spend more time and attention with their products. These "attention engineers" have devised such ways as rewarding users who consistently use a product over many days. Many employers are now realizing that improper uses of computers are actually hindering efficiency and productivity in many workplaces.

In looking at the challenges associated with using screens well, parents may be tempted to simply opt to do away with all or nearly all screen use in their families. This may be the right thing for some families, especially if prudent restraint is not practical for whatever reason. But most parents recognize that computers offer benefits as well as challenges. Many are looking for guidance on how to help their children grow up learning how to properly use this technology. The following are some suggested steps that parents can take, in order of importance:

- Use screens only in public places. Children should never have access to screens that can connect to the Internet in privacy. Family computers should be located on desks or counters, positioned so that the screens are visible to members of the family in the most public areas of the home. This is particularly challenging with laptops, tablets, and smartphones. The term "phone" is actually not very accurate to describe the handheld devices that people typically carry today. Compared to the time spent using these devices for email, social media, texting, GPS, games, and surfing the Internet, the time spent talking on them as phones is limited. Smart "phones" are computers, not phones. The complications that arise when unlimited and apparently anonymous access to the Internet is given to adolescents are quite significant. Obviously, not all the content on the Internet is appropriate for young people (or anyone) to view. I know that when I was an adolescent, I would not have been able to consistently resist natural boyhood curiosity if I had been given this type of access. It is not fair to burden young people with the responsibility of avoiding images that are so readily accessible on their mobile devices in apparent privacy. Even if there was a way to avoid this problem, it is difficult for young people to grow in the virtues highlighted above if they have constant access to the online world. Limited access is a necessary, but not sufficient, condition for helping people to properly use this powerful technology rather than be used by it.

• Use screens in culturally enriching ways as a family. Computers can be used well to facilitate communication, to access information, and to tap cultural riches. Parents should take the lead in fostering and modeling their proper use. This will help children internalize a vision for the proper use of screens in general. Parents may use the computer to Skype with relatives, instructing the children to sit quietly until asked a question or until they have a positive contribution to make to the conversation. Plan a family movie night where the family watches a well-chosen film. Use the computer to work on a family project, such as producing an annual Christmas letter that includes photos and stories about the family. Play edifying music through the computer while doing family chores. Listen to educational podcasts or video lectures. Hear classic books read by talented narrators. All of these will help children use technology in humanly enriching ways.

- No video games. Sensible parents teach their children that computers are useful professional tools, helpful to access information and some cultural material. In contrast, the typical video game is designed to captivate the gamer, isolating him or her from authentic human interactions. In the world of the video game, the player passes the time, entertained and distracted from the

stress and boredom of ordinary life. With
the possible exception of more social video
games such as some of the group activities designed for the Wii gaming system,
video games generally lack the characteris-
tics that make childhood play a healthy and
positive way to spend time. Authentic play
includes one or more of the following elements: an active imagination, physical activity, and social interaction. Video games that
lack these elements are more like a system
designed to alleviate boredom than something that enables real play. Time is a trea-
sure, a great gift we have been given that is
meant to be sanctified, to be spent in purposeful ways. We can choose to fill our
free time in various goal-oriented pursuits:
acts of service, learning a foreign language,
developing a skill, or even reflective thinking, to name only a few. Any use of time
that is intended to escape reality, to medicate boredom by simply passing the time,
is contrary to the true meaning of the great
gift of time that we have been given. To

seek an escape from reality through a video game is a form of practical nihilism; it is asserting with how one chooses to spend time that there is no meaning in the time that passes. Playing a video game typically leaves the person empty afterward, opening up a new boredom that should be a gentle reminder that we are made for so much more. Unfortunately, many instead try to escape this discomfort through patterns of reality avoidance that, if not checked, can lead to further addictions.

• Set times when screens are not used. All computers should be shut down after a certain time at night, not to be turned on until the next morning. It also may make sense, depending on the family culture, to have other screen-free times during the day.

• Flip phones for children. It is very convenient to be able to call or text a child. Also, many social events are planned and communicated through text messages. Some parents allow children to own flip phones or other simple phones since these devices do not present the same challenges associated with smart phones. Even so, these phones should be collected at a certain time each evening. Children should not have phones with them during the night.

- Keep screens out of the hands of toddlers and young children. It is completely unnecessary to give a young child access to a tablet or smart "phone," even if it is to do something apparently harmless or even meaningful. At a young age, children develop best by interacting with reality rather than screens.

- Monitor use of social media. Parents should carefully regulate the use of social media by their teenage children. It is best for parents to be connected to any social media that teenage children use. Not all social media are the same. Using Facebook to plan an event with friends is very different from the type of connectivity promoted by such applications as Snapchat. In general, social media use should be consistent with that of computers placed in public family places.

- Employ filters and parental controls. Use filters and parental controls, but keep in mind that these are of limited effectiveness. If you doubt this, ask a typical teenager if you are wise to place significant trust in these systems. At best, filters and parental controls can help to keep an honest child honest. An important note is that Google makes significant profits each year from the porn industry. There is no way to remove the browser from any of their Android phones. Furthermore, it is impossible to block porn images even with the best filters in Google search. (The browser can be removed on an iPhone.)

- Laptops, tablets, and smart phones are for adults. Strength of character is what makes an adult. It is possible, although truly exceptional, for someone to be an adult today as early as fifteen years old. Parents know when their child is so strongly formed, so strongly committed to living a God-centered life of service to others, that he or she is an adult in all things except experience. Hopefully a child will reach this point before he or she departs for college. If so, then it is not a bad idea to allow the child to have his or her own laptop, tablet, or smart phone a few months before leaving for college. For the sake of the other children, however, it is best to hold off on allowing this until shortly before departure, even for the truly exceptional younger adult.

CHAPTER FOUR

The Final Cause

Forming Authentic Freedom

The final cause of a thing is that for which it comes to be, the end for which it has been designed. It is easy to see how final causality is present in man-made artifacts. A chair is designed for sitting, a car is built for efficient and pleasant transportation, and a house is built for shelter. It is obvious that chairs, cars, and houses are built for reasons, and that these reasons inform the way each thing is constructed. Those who build a house keep in mind the family who will live there, both in the overall architectural design of the house to suit a particular family's needs and in the fine detail work, as when a carpenter installs a cabinet with an eye to how each detail of his work will appear to the new owners. It would not be sensible for someone to construct a random artifact for no purpose whatsoever. It is obvious that the final cause, that for which a thing comes to be, informs the entire process of crafting something.

Final causality is also present in nature, especially in living things that act for certain ends. In nature, however, the final cause is something that is sought as perfecting a thing's given nature in some way. The nature of a thing comes from what it is, from its form. Thus formal and final causality are closely related in natural things acting to fulfill what they are. A tree grows tall and spreads its branches far and wide, seeking the sunlight necessary for it to grow and the perfection of being a mature tree. A squirrel gathers acorns to store for the winter, trying to ensure his survival when food is difficult to find. And a mother bear cares for her cubs, seeking both the natural growth and thriving of her offspring and a fulfillment of her nature as a mother.

The specific dignity of the human person is that not only do we act in ways that further our natural development, but that each person is able to freely choose to do so, participating in his or her perfection with both reason and will. This freedom is precisely what enables men and women to choose a difficult course of action for a greater, even a transcendent, good. Even the most loyal dog, which would recklessly charge a bear to defend its master, is not capable of stopping itself from eating readily available food when hungry. A person, however, can choose to forgo food and other elements necessary for survival for the sake of a greater good. There was once a starving prisoner who, when given a bowl of soup by his jailers, ate most of the bowl but returned the final third or so to the guards. He later told how by this action he preserved his dignity as an interiorly free man, despite the degrading situation he was in.

The final cause of a parent's efforts to raise his children is that they become mature adults, with strong characters, focused on living God-centered and other-centered lives. As we have seen, the virtues are of great importance, as that through which a person's character is forged. By acquiring the virtues, a person grows into a man or woman of strong character. But the virtues are not static habits that are ends in themselves. The virtues are meant to be freely exercised to accomplish good. Freedom is a necessary condition for virtue to be alive and active. Without a true spirit of freedom there can be no authentic virtue. At best there may be a semblance of virtue, something that appears to be properly ordered, but in reality is only so as long as proper conditions are present. When people find themselves truly on their own, in situations in which they need to exercise their own freedom, as, for example, a freshman living away from home at college, character that is not authentic can easily fall sway to various pressures.

The key is to raise adults who will carry within themselves their own environment, a moral environment forged by a free and mature commitment to what is right. Such young adults will transform the environment in which they find themselves rather than be transformed by it. A parent who has raised such a child sends him or her off to college mostly with confidence and joy, knowing that he or she will take advantage of the good opportunities present and help others to likewise live good lives. I write "mostly" because informed parents know that the college environment is particularly challenging and that it can be difficult at times even for morally strong young adults. Parents who are aware of the challenges that arise when eighteen- to twenty-two-year-olds are away from their families in a very different living environment will continue to support their college children with lots of intercessory prayer.

But how do parents help their children to grow in true freedom? How do parents ensure that the virtues they begin to teach, by stories that inform the moral imagination and by directed practice, take root deeply in their children? A large part of the answer is to have confidence in what constitutes the good for a human being; in other words, having confidence in what we are made for. Each person has been created by God to be a saint, to be a close friend of God, in and through his or her ordinary life and duties. God wants his friends to reach the perfection of charity, carrying his love throughout the world as the one true light that can transform any environment. Sanctity is not just for those with a special calling to separate themselves from the world, expressly chosen and consecrated for a particular service. Sanctity is what all men and women are called to pursue— in their college dorms, in their studies, in their families, and in their professional work.

Parents who have confidence that their children have been made for nothing less than to be saints have a tremendous appreciation for the natural teleology, the final causality, that is built into our natures. St. Augustine said it well when he noted at the beginning of his *Confessions* that God has made us for himself and our hearts are restless until they rest in him. Nothing in this world can fully satisfy the human heart. The heart will always long for more, and its dignity is to continue to move forward on a quest for the love of God, the only thing that can satisfy man. Granted, there are no saints here on earth. On earth there are only those of us who struggle on our journey, moving from the great victory God has already won in Christ toward the full realization of this victory with him in heaven.

And on this quest, each step is worked out amid various material details and circumstances. We all long for lesser goods, many of which have value and should be seen as gifts from God. We follow a particular path with very human concerns constantly before us. We work at a myriad of tasks and serve in innumerable ways. From the child at play, building a house of blocks, to the mature adult helping others through professional work, we move toward our final end in steps and through life's material and temporal details.

From this it follows that parents must protect and foster the freedom of their children to advance on this journey. Wise parents know that their children's hearts have been made with longings for the good, for what leads beyond themselves, eventually toward the greatest Good, God himself. Parents need to see part of their role as keeping their children on this noble quest, helping to set up the conditions for free action and growth. Granted, hearts wounded by sin can easily be distracted by lesser goods or even by things that are harmful. But parents can usually discern when their children are seeking something that is detrimental. The role of parents is to be discerning, understanding the hearts of their children and striving to keep them on the noble quest for that for which they have been made.

Discerning matters of the heart and fostering freedom in children are not always easy tasks. Here are some practical thoughts on how parents can do this:

- Unstructured time is a must. It is a critical mistake to overly manage children's schedules to the point where they are shuffled from activity to activity without being allowed to decide for themselves how to use their time. Overmanaging children makes it difficult for them to develop the habit of freely committing to a good, a necessary condition for true virtue to develop. Having unstructured time, time that children have to decide for themselves how to use, forces them to exercise their freedom. When there is not anything specifically planned for them, they must decide for themselves what to do. Granted, a good family schedule includes lots of time set aside for specific purposes such as meals, chores, various activities, and even quiet reading or study. But even in a busy day there should be some unstructured time, and on a typical weekend day, for example, there should be several hours of it.

- Do not allow entertainment that stifles the expression of your child's personality. The most common argument for reducing unstructured time as much as possible is that children tend to waste this time or use it badly. Parents observe that when left on their own, children tend to get into trouble, perhaps through arguing or fighting with one another. Or they tend to gravitate toward some mindless form of entertainment that is, at best, a complete waste of time. This is not surprising. Sensible parents know that it can be difficult to exercise one's freedom to commit to seeking a good. It may be easier for a young boy to amuse himself by tormenting his sister than by joining with her in some form of creative play. And the easiest thing of all might be for him to pass the time playing video games. There is a natural human tendency to seek some form of entertainment to fill down time. Aristotle noted that this is the case, and even observed that the majority of people never get past this slavish existence. He wrote, "The utter servility of the masses comes out in their preference for a bovine existence."[1] To seek gratification of our basic appetites, as opposed to seeking higher things through virtuous action, is to live a cow-like existence that is below the dignity of free men. One of the most important ways that parents can foster true freedom in their children is, from a very young age, to deliberately remove as many forms of distracting, personality-stifling entertainment as possible. The key is to be discerning. Wholesome entertainment is fine when enjoyed in moderation. There is no harm in two young siblings building a structure out of Legos, for

---

1. Aristotle, *Nicomachean Ethics*, trans. J.A.K. Thomson (New York: Penguin, 1976), p. 68.

example. Parents need to become attuned to perceive the difference between toys that children use in creative, imaginative play and things designed to captivate the attention of children so as to pass the time. Perhaps it is best to think about such things as falling on a spectrum. A natural object like a stick has no particular captivating powers of its own. Children will use sticks in play; but in doing so they are themselves determining how to use the sticks, whether to build a fort or use them as imaginary swords, as bats in a game of stick ball, as tools to help climb a tree, or even as projectiles. Legos are different in that they are an artificial system. While an argument could be made that Legos are not as good as natural construction materials, it is nonetheless the case that Legos are primarily passive units to which the child has to add form. Legos allow for a fair amount of creativity. Similarly, dress-up clothes can be very helpful for little children to enter into creative and imaginative play. As mentioned above, however, many uses of screens are not like this.

Certain films and video games are designed to captivate the viewer, engulfing his or her personality and absorbing freedom rather than allowing true freedom to grow. Just as the Lord demanded that the children of Israel have no strange gods before him—that they smash all idols—so parents analogously need to "smash" all things that engulf their children's freedom. Practically, this means letting grandparents and relatives know that you do not want electronic gadgets for Christmas and birthday presents. It means getting rid of that obnoxious beeping baby toy right away and never letting video games in your house. It means watching carefully how your children play with what they have, being ready to take away anything that threatens to distract your child from the quest they are on to use their freedom for the good. One of my sons became totally engrossed in a spherical puzzle ball toy called a Perplexus. With no video games allowed in our home, this became his substitute. It was difficult to take this away from him and get rid of it. He felt a real sense of loss, which made life more difficult for the rest of the family for the short term. Even so, it was not long before his heart was directed to other, much better interests. Considering the affluence of our times, I would go so far as to say that it is nothing short of heroic for parents not to spoil their children today. But we need such heroic parents!

- Boredom is often your ally. If parents do a good job of removing captivating forms of entertainment meant to engross attention and pass the time, children inevitably will complain of being bored. Parents who hear their children complain about boredom should first of all congratulate themselves. They are doing something profoundly right in not allowing this boredom to be "medicated away" by captivating entertainment. A great response to a child complaining of boredom could be something like, "You're bored. That's great! I can't wait to see what you will decide to do next." Granted, if the complaints of boredom get too annoying, a sensible parent will respond by giving the child a chore to do. But fundamentally, boredom is a mild form of suffering that opens up the possibility of creative play, constructive action, and an authentic exercise of human freedom. In a society like ours, where most of one's material needs are nearly always satisfied, boredom is a great ally to parents hoping their children will freely embrace the good. It is out of boredom that healthy play and great childhood adventures are born.

- Tolerating messes. Unstructured time in an environment free from various distractions does come with challenges. Children often embark upon crazy and messy endeavors. Our children have made our backyard interesting with their "structures" and forts, some in trees, some on the ground, and some underground. Two of our children once dug a hole in our backyard so deep that progress was only being made by one passing a bucket of dirt up to the other to empty. (When they decided to tunnel sideways, I knew the project had to stop for safety reasons.) Our daughters have "decorated" our house with pictures and other crafts on birthdays and other occasions, their way of trying to make our house a welcoming home. Parents need to become comfortable with this state of affairs. Children grow a great deal through exercising virtues during play. When left on their own, they naturally develop a variety of games and activities that are not only expressions of their freedom but also catalysts for exercising other virtues. They prudently decide the rule for what constitutes a ground rules double on an odd-shaped stickball lot. They learn about leadership as they figure out how to organize themselves into teams. At The Heights School, which I described earlier as the all-boys school where I work, there are intentionally unstructured times of play, especially for the Lower School boys (grades 3–5) whose domain is a wooded valley. They build forts out of sticks, trees, rocks, and other odd objects found in the valley. There is a mostly friendly rivalry as the boys work out their own political system of which forts are "against" each other.

- Fostering the noble quest. If children are in the habit of exercising their freedom in childhood play, it is likely that they will, as they get older, seek out greater adventures that involve planning and effort. A few years ago, our older three boys asked for permission to ride bikes from our home in Rockville, Maryland, to Harpers Ferry, West Virginia. After hearing them out, we allowed them to go on this overnight adventure. They camped along the Appalachian Trail and returned the next day. The following year they did a six-day backpacking trip in the Shenandoah Mountains, camping in hammocks and seeing several bears. These same boys formed a thriving business by dressing up in nice clothes and going door to door throughout our neighborhood with business cards, seeking work mowing lawns and doing other yard jobs.

Parenting this way is certainly messy and at times inefficient. But despite the complications, encouraging your children to exercise freedom will lead them to internalize a strong sense of responsibility. Even in grade school, our oldest three children have always taken complete responsibility for their academic work. Angela and I have had little no involvement in their day–to-day academic tasks. If anything, we have made it more difficult for them by adding family responsibilities—chores and looking after younger siblings—to their already demanding academic responsibilities. All three are outstanding students. Michael and Thomas are currently excelling in their studies at The University of Notre Dame, and Theresa is thriving in her senior year of high school at Oakcrest School, an independent Catholic school for girls.

Conclusion

————— • ◆ • —————

I n times past, families lived more rooted lives. It was common to dwell in the same town all one's life, learning in a natural way from strong family and community relationships. Grandparents shared important wisdom with their adult children, and the broader community supported individual families. Perhaps there was a church in the center of town that served as a focal point for unifying the community.

While we can long for a simpler time when lives were more connected to a particular place, the reality today is that we live in a highly mobile society. Even though it is not always possible, it is good if children settle close to their parents. There are significant benefits when multiple generations of families live close enough to support and learn from one another. When circumstances require distance, some adult children try to visit their parents in their childhood homes with a fair amount of frequency. And regardless of distance, most parents recognize that there is a sense in which it is good that their adult children are independent. It is a positive and natural happening for them to make their own ways in the world. Indeed, if children remain living at home for too long, this can be a source of anxiety, as parents long for the day when their children will be more independent.

Our highly mobile and technologically interconnected society is not without its benefits. People today have easy access to cultural riches that would have astounded our ancestors. Technology makes it possible to network with individuals throughout the world: one's work can have a tremendous impact not just on one's immediate community but also on many others. Today there are vast horizons of work to be done in diverse areas of culture. There is a need for men and women to humanize the structures of our modern world so that they serve the human person. There is a need to produce new art that fosters beauty and connectedness to reality. There is a need for genuine collaboration between peoples who refuse to limit themselves to only considering technical soundness, but who instead seek solutions that foster the integral development of the human person as well. If we fail at this task, the result will be impersonal structures that consume humanity, treating individuals as mere functional productive units. We will be reduced to cogs in a machine.

The biggest parental challenge resulting from the pace and forms of modern life is that it is more difficult for wisdom and perspective to be organically passed from one generation to the next. Young parents struggle with challenges that could easily be solved by advice from more experienced parents or grandparents. Even though the dispersion and pace of modern life have made this more difficult, it is possible to study parenting challenges today to gain perspective so as to make better decisions. It is my hope that this book has been useful in furthering such reflection and study.

The job of being a parent is never easy. I mentioned that my wife and I have felt like soldiers in the trenches, not knowing how the overall battle is going. Each child is unique, and the challenges each one faces in growing up, while similar in some respects, are never exactly the same. It is simply the lot of parents to struggle daily, to pray for their children, and to frequently study and reflect on their own family situation and each child to the point where this prayerful reflection is habitual. St. Josemaría Escrivá offered a wonderful image for such daily struggle. He saw our ongoing labors as analogous to those of a donkey at a waterwheel, laboring to turn the wheel round and round so as to pump water to irrigate arid land. The donkey perseveres at his humble task, knowing nothing of the lush fruitfulness that results from his labors.

Occasionally, however, parents do catch glimpses of the fruits of their labors, even when their children are young. And there comes a time when parents know that their work is mostly complete, that they have raised a responsible adult ready to play his or her part in transforming the world. For Angela and me, the previous two graduations from The Heights School were such occasions. One distinctive aspect of a Heights graduation is that when presenting the diplomas, the headmaster, currently Alvaro de Vicente, personally comments on each of the sixty or so graduates. As the head of the Upper School, my role is a ceremonial one; as one of three others, along with the assistant headmaster and the chaplain, I sit on the stage, shake hands, and listen.

When my son Michael graduated in 2016, Alvaro mentioned, among other points, the backpacking trip my older sons embarked upon for six days in the Shenandoah Mountains. Though Thomas later complained that Mr. de Vicente made it sound like his older brother Michael— only older by sixteen months—was babysitting him, Alvaro accurately highlighted how responsible Michael was. Alvaro went on to note that Michael not only could be counted on to look out for others on such a trip but that he was the one senior Alvaro would be comfortable placing in charge of a group of his peers. Shortly afterward, Alvaro graciously passed to me the responsibility of awarding Michael his diploma. I was so proud of my son and Michael was so moved that it was little surprise that we together managed to drop the diploma instead of passing it off smoothly, adding a bit of delightful humor to an already wonderful day.

The following year it was Thomas's turn. I had the great privilege not only of successfully passing Thomas his diploma but also of listening to him deliver his speech as valedictorian. As he spoke, I was reflecting on the times he had found ways of getting into trouble in the past. He was the boy I sent to sit in the corner at home after misbehaving during Mass, although he remembers the incident a bit differently. He frequently argued with me about everything from our family schedule to how to properly interpret Aristotle's claims about friendship. I was reflecting that though Thomas seemed to enjoy arguing for the sake of arguing, he really was deeply internalizing what he came to recognize was the truth. Indeed, I could not help realizing that his speech was a powerful affirmation of the education he had received at home and at The Heights School. Shortly, he would be off to join his brother Michael at Notre Dame, and I could not have been prouder as his father. Thomas's speech, most of which is reproduced here with his permission, is a fitting apologetic for authentic freedom and shows just how much children internalize what their parents, at times with little grace, imperfectly teach them:

Thomas Moynihan
Valedictorian Speech

Many people in our world today possess a loose notion that freedom allows someone to do whatever they want, that freedom poses no restrictions but only limitless options. Further reflection, however, reveals that there are right and wrong choices and that no one who continually chooses evil can remain free. With that in mind, let's look at two types of freedom, both external and internal. External freedom involves how we relate physically to the world around us. It is manifested by physical movement. Internal freedom involves how we relate to ourselves. It is manifested by mental self-movement, exercised through the stable habits or virtues that enable one to choose the good.

External freedom does not always look like an important component of a school. Some might find it difficult to see how freedom of movement is an integral aspect of education. There is, however, something about boys, especially younger boys, that begs for freedom to explore nature. Before I came to The Heights as a third grader, I was always intrigued by nature and the outdoors. My brothers and I would go on short bike rides or hikes almost daily. We just loved exploring. Coming to The Heights made this whole pursuit much easier. As students, we were given freedom to explore the valley, climb trees, have snowball fights, and much more. I remember one day in the middle of fourth grade; it had rained heavily the entire previous night. When we finally reached school, it was still pouring rain. The valley, where all the lower school classes take place, has two pits, the upper pit and lower pit, and both had flooded. There were at least a full four to five feet of water in the lower pit, and it looked like a small pond. Rather than wait inside for the downpour to pass, we had the idea of lashing huge logs beneath a large slab of plywood to create a raft. We used two 2 x 6 boards to sail around in the water until school started. We did, of course, fall off several times and become soaked, but even though we had to live with wet clothes for a few hours, we still enjoyed the experience thoroughly.

Middle school saw the continuation of our fascination with nature. The fishpond next to the middle school building has a pump system so that it flows continuously. Because of the flowing water, the pond rarely freezes completely. One side might be frozen several solid inches down while the other side has merely a thin glaze of ice. When this occurred, there were invariably those of us who tried to go as far out on the ice as possible without breaking through. Half the time they would crash through the ice anyway, soaking themselves up to their waists in freezing water. Mr. Reed's office is adjacent to the fishpond, and he could have put an end to our escapades at any time, but instead chose to just watch us, allowing our own imprudence to teach us instead. Similar methods were used throughout our education. When one student asked if he should eat a raw oyster on our third-grade camping trip, he was advised not to by the teachers. He chose to do so anyway, and his mistake became his teacher. This sort of hands-off approach to regulation is very much a part of The Heights. Students are given a great deal of external freedom.

Internal freedom, however, is far more important. It is not possible to regulate internal freedom in the same way as external freedom because someone's choices are deeply personal and one's own. Advice can be given, but in the end, no one can choose for someone else. There is a dichotomy between the world's idea of freedom and the true idea of freedom. Freedom is the ability to choose the good rather than just to do whatever one wants. In eighth grade, I remember debating this very topic. We came up with several examples in which choosing evil led to dependence on something, thereby reducing freedom. We were able to reason for ourselves that freedom is the ability to choose the good rather than simply have the teacher tell us so. This method of dialogue within classes leads to an informed but also self-reasoned system of belief.

The dialogic style of classroom discussion, however, also provides ample opportunities to reveal the students who aren't putting in the work. In tenth grade, Mr. Bissex was my teacher for first-period English. A few students were late to class fairly often, and there was a significant chance that they did not read the assigned material. When class began, we would collaborate with Mr. Bissex, who would make an outlandish claim involving the characters in the reading, and then would ask the certain late student if he agreed and if so, to comment on the assertion. That student would then generally proceed to agree in as detached a way as possible, steering clear of any facts and ending up conveying nonsense to hide the fact that he hadn't read. The practical joke wasn't malicious, but rather friendly. The students who didn't read were given a compelling reason to do so without really being punished. Punishments aren't always a deterrent, but humiliation, even slight and good-natured humiliation, almost always is.

In ways such as these, The Heights helps, but does not force, its students to choose the good. Another major way that The Heights fosters this true idea of freedom as choosing the good is through its advisory program. Students in each grade are paired with a faculty member who aims to assist them in four major areas of life: academic, social, athletic, and spiritual. Any questions or concerns that a student has can be brought up in advisory, and the advisor finishes by helping the student to make several goals. Through this program and through its teaching methods, a Heights education really does help a student to know the good, and hopefully to choose it as well. Freedom is, I believe, an integral aspect of a Heights education and what sets The Heights apart from so many other schools.

The Heights has been an incredible benefit to me and my classmates. We are very grateful to our parents, teachers, and coaches who have helped us to be where we are today. The education we have received will aid us well in college and beyond. But above that, The Heights has prepared us for life and its various difficulties and hardships. With all that being said, it is clear how much The Heights has given us. How are we going to give back to The Heights? . . . Above all, we need to take what we have been given and carry the mission of The Heights to our colleges, workplaces, and beyond. Classes such as History of Western Thought and Apologetics have given us the tools to think clearly, to recognize many of the flaws with modern thought and hopefully to help correct them, and ultimately to become truly free.

Postscript—August 2018

As I write this, my older children have just started classes in college: Michael and Thomas at Notre

Dame—as a junior and a sophomore, respectively, and Theresa as a freshman at The University of Dallas. The rest of the family is getting ready for school to start. Angela and I are back to the day-to-day adventure of trying to care for and educate the eight children still under our roof, as well as supporting our older children with friendship and prayers from a distance.

There seems to be no end to the constant material details that need attention, as the ebb and flow between chaos and order continues on a daily basis. Angela and I are finding out every day just how different each child is, as we see that what worked for one does not always meet the needs of the others. And the richness of family life offers no lack of opportunities for revealing the personal defects of the members, parents included.

Not too long ago my oldest daughter, Theresa, gave me one of the best corrections I have ever received. I was raising my voice in my effort to get a point across. At times our house can be loud, and it is easy for parents and others to fall into the habit of speaking loudly, sometimes necessarily so. Later, Theresa privately cautioned me about making corrections in a loud voice to my daughters. She observed that from her younger sister Elizabeth's perspective, Dad was yelling at her. She noted that a daughter can be more sensitive to this than a son and that the relationship of a father to his daughters is different than to his sons. I thanked her for her correction and have tried to keep it in mind ever since. But I was also proud of her for the way she handled this with maturity and strength.

So much of family life is about having the humility to recognize our failings and to apologize—and to keep a sense of humor. It is certainly true that parents today need to exercise decisive leadership. Children need parents who deeply reflect on the awesome challenges and opportunities facing families today, and then take the right strong steps. But none of us are perfect. We are all flawed human beings, with faults that we see and faults that are perhaps apparent to others but hidden to us. The best families are not those without any problems. And growing up in a peaceful, protected environment free from all conflict is not what is best for children either. Children thrive when they see and experience challenges that are overcome. It is families that have the resources to stay together and struggle through difficulties that forge virtue in their children.

It is not a problem that there are no perfect families. The hope of our times is the family that strives to become more of the "communion of persons" that it is called to be, to use the sage words of St. John Paul II. We as parents will be successful not to the extent that our families have the appearance of perfection, we will be successful to the extent that we accept, embrace, and work through the difficulties and challenges of family life in our particular situations.

We can always count on God's grace. And God is not expecting us to immediately overcome our flaws, root out all discord in our families, and achieve harmony. Rather, he is eager to accompany us both when things go well and we are filled with joy and gratitude, and also as we struggle and rise after our many falls and disappointments. And he has worked it out such that our faithful struggle, with a sporting spirit toward life's challenges and our very real personal limitations, is what our children *really* need from us.